FELIPPI WYSSEN

Diese Buchreihe versammelt die Bauwerke einzelner, mit hohem Qualitätsanspruch ausgewählter jüngerer Schweizer Architekten. Seit 2004 kuratiere ich die Reihe *Anthologie* in der Form einfacher Werkdokumentationen. Sie ist vergleichbar mit der «Blütenlese», wie sie in der Literatur für eine Sammlung ausgewählter Texte angewendet wird. Es liegt in der Natur des Architektenberufs, dass die Erstlingswerke junger Architekten meist kleinere übersichtliche Bauaufgaben sind. Sie sind eine Art Fingerübung, mit der die Architekten das Erlernte anwenden und ihr architektonisches Sensorium erproben und entfalten können. Die Begabung und die Leidenschaft für das Metier lassen sich dabei früh in voller Deutlichkeit und Frische erkennen. So stecken in jedem der kleinen und grossen Projekte inspirierte Grundgedanken und Vorstellungen, die spielerisch und gleichermassen perfekt in architektonische Bilder, Formen und Räume umgesetzt werden. Damit wird mir wieder einmal bewusst, dass in der Architektur wie in anderen Kunstformen die Bilder und Ideen, die hinter dem Werk stehen, das Wesentliche sind. Es mag diese Intuition sein, die der Künstler hat, und die dann über sein Werk wie ein Funke auf den Betrachter überspringt, so wie es der italienische Philosoph Benedetto Croce in seinen Schriften eindringlich beschreibt.

Heinz Wirz
Verleger

This book series presents buildings by selected young Swiss architects that set themselves high quality standards. Since 2004, i had been curating the *Anthologie* series by simply documenting their oeuvre. The series can be compared to a literary anthology presenting a collection of selected texts. It is in the nature of the architectural profession that early works by young architects are mostly small, limited building tasks. They are a kind of five-finger exercise in which the architects apply what they have learnt, as well as testing and developing their architectural instincts. Talent and a passion for the profession can clearly be seen at an early stage in all of its clarity and freshness. Each project, be it large or small, contains an inspired underlying concept and ideas that are playfully and consummately implemented as architectural images, forms and spaces. Thus, I am regularly reminded that in architecture, as in other art forms, the images and ideas behind the works are their essence. Perhaps this is the same intuition described so vividly by the Italian philosopher Benedetto Croce, one that is absorbed by the artist and flies like a spark via the work to the viewer.

Heinz Wirz
Publisher

FELIPPI WYSSEN

Quart Verlag

BAUERNHAUS, ADLISWIL
Ausführung 2012–2013

Das Bauernhaus aus dem 16. Jahrhundert besteht aus einem Teil zum Wohnen und dem Tenn. Eine «Wanne» in Holzbauweise überspannt in Längsrichtung das Tenn. Beim Betreten des Gebäudes tritt die Wanne als geometrisches Element in Erscheinung und bewahrt die ursprüngliche Grosszügigkeit des Tenns. Vom Eingang führt eine Art Weg durch das Gebäude, der sich je nach Funktion ausweitet und Raum für unterschiedliche Nutzungen wie Garderobe, Bibliothek und Arbeiten schafft. Im Dachgeschoss gelangt man in die Wanne – eine Wohn-, Ess- und Küchenlandschaft auf verschiedenen Niveaus. Dachstuhl und Wanne rahmen das Panorama prismatisch. Eine Bodenluke im Wohnbereich schafft die räumliche Verbindung zum Tenn und schliesst den Rundgang ab.

FARMHOUSE, ADLISWIL
Construction 2012–2013

The 16th-century farmhouse consists of a living area and a barn. A timber basin spans the barn longitudinally. On entering the building, the basin appears as a new, geometric building element and retains the original spacious character of the barn. From the entrance, visitors follow a route through the building that broadens depending on its utilisation, providing space for a wide range of uses such as a wardrobe, library and an office. The basin creates a loft space with a living, dining and kitchen landscape on several levels, whereby the roof structure and the basin prismatically frame the panorama view. An incision in the living area's floor creates a spatial connection to the barn and concludes the circular route through the building.

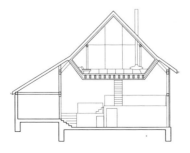

10 m

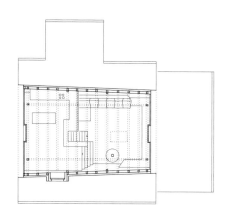

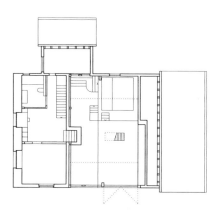

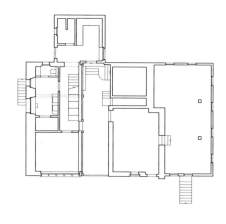

10 m

8

WOHNHAUS BASELSTRASSE, MUTTENZ
Ausführung 2013–2015

Der Baukörper dieses Wohnhauses liegt auf einer ins Terrain eingesenkten Parzelle. Die zeichenhafte Südfassade und das allseitig auskragende Satteldach verleihen dem Bau seinen bodenständigen Charakter. Deutlich abgesetzte Horizontalzonen bestimmen die Schauseiten: der teils verborgene Sockel, das grosszügig geöffnete Obergeschoss und das elegant eingeschnittene Dach. Feine Profile und plastische Interventionen akzentuieren die Fassaden, während Parkettböden und Schiebeläden den Gegenpart zum Sichtbeton bilden.

Spannung erhält das Bauvolumen durch den Wechsel zwischen Loggien und Innenräumen. Raumhohe Türen und Durchgänge schaffen Blickachsen und ein reizvolles Raumkontinuum.

RESIDENTIAL BUILDING IN BASELSTRASSE, MUTTENZ
Construction 2013–2015

The volume of this residential building is situated on a plot that has been sunken into the terrain. The symbolic south façade and the saddle roof, which projects on all sides, give the structure a down-to-earth character. Clearly detached horizontal zones define the visible façades: the partially hidden base, the generously open upper level and the elegantly incised roof. Fine profiles and sculptural interventions accentuate the façades, while the parquet flooring and sliding shutters form a counterpart to the fair-faced concrete.

The building volume gains its tension through the alternation between the loggias and the interior spaces. Room-high doors and passages create visual axes and an attractive spatial continuum.

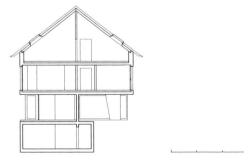

10 m

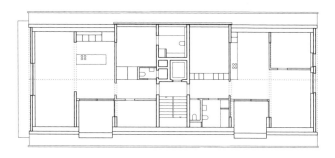

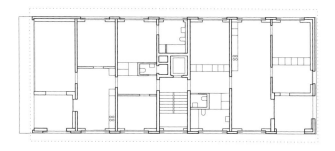

10 m

16

WOHNHAUS GATTERNWEG, RIEHEN
Ausführung 2016–2018

Nicht nur der Baukörper, sondern auch die Oberflächen und Grundrisslösungen unterscheiden sich von dem umgebenden Bestand. Entscheidend für das dennoch verträgliche Einpassen des Neubaus ist das nach oben kräftig zurückgestufte Volumen: Aufgrund dieser dynamischen Reduktion des «Footprints» wirkt es optisch leichter; zugleich entstehen an den Schmalseiten grosszügige Terrassen.

Alle Fassaden sind kontrastierend zur grünen Umgebung mit schwarz geöltem Fichtenholz verkleidet. Zusammen mit den wandhohen Schlagläden geben sie dem Bau etwas Archaisches und spielen mit dem Erscheinungsbild ländlicher Infrastrukturbauten.

RESIDENTIAL BUILDING IN GATTERNWEG, RIEHEN
Construction 2016–2018

Not only the building volume, but also the surfaces and floor plan solutions differ from the existing neighbouring structures. However, the decisive factor for the new building's harmonious integration is its strongly recessed volume, which is staggered as it ascends: this dynamic reduction of its footprint makes the volume visually lighter; at the same time, it creates spacious terraces on its narrow sides.

All façades contrast with the green surroundings through their black oiled spruce wood. Together with the wall-high shutters, they give the building an archaic quality and play on the appearance of rural infrastructural buildings.

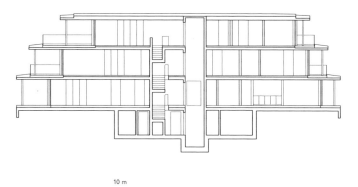

10 m

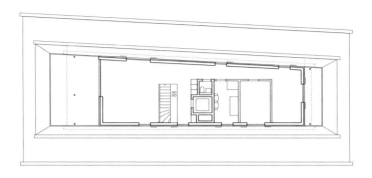

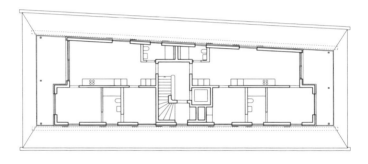

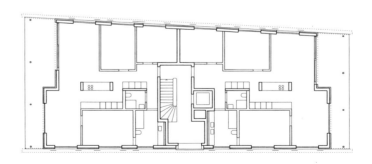

10 m

24

WOHNHAUS RUPPEN, MUTTENZ
Ausführung 2016–2018

Während das bestehende Gebäude modernisiert wurde, brachte eine behutsam ausgeführte Erweiterung auf der Gartenseite des Hauses zusätzlichen Wohnraum. Die nur 1.80 Meter schmale neue Raumschicht, die sich über die gesamte Breite des Gebäudes zieht, verdoppelt die Nutzfläche der dort vorhandenen Zimmer beinahe. Dieser kleine Eingriff ermöglichte die strukturelle Entflechtung der bestehenden Räume und Nutzungen, zugleich verleiht er dem Erdgeschoss des Gebäudes eine neue Grosszügigkeit. Die über die ganze Fassadenbreite geführte Holztreppe im Freien bildet neu einen ungekünstelten Übergang zwischen Wohnhaus und Garten, der auch als Sitzplatz seine Qualitäten entfaltet.

RUPPEN RESIDENTIAL BUILDING, MUTTENZ
Construction 2016–2018

While the existing building was being modernised, a gently implemented extension on the house's garden side provided additional living space. The new layer, which is only 1.80 metres wide and covers the entire breadth of the building, almost doubles the usable space of the existing rooms. This small measure made it possible to dissolve the structure of the existing rooms and uses, while also giving the ground floor a new spaciousness. The wooden outdoor stairs leading over the entire breadth of the façade creates an authentic transition between the home and the garden, which also develops its qualities as a place to sit.

5 m

WOHNHAUS MOOSWEG, RIEHEN
Ausführung 2017–2019

Auffälligstes Merkmal dieses zweigeschossigen Neubaus ist die Dachlandschaft, die die verschiedenen Nutzungszonen im Inneren nach aussen zeigt. Während das Hauptdach die Wohn-, Ess- und Schlafräume unter sich vereint, markiert das über der schmalen Terrasse platzierte Vordach den Übergang zwischen Haus und Garten, und unter dem schmalen rückwärtigen Dach verbergen sich alle Funktions- und Erschliessungsräume. Im Inneren des in Holzleichtbauweise ausgeführten Nullenergie-Hauses durchdringen sich zwei Schichtungen: Neben der von den Wohngeschossen geprägten horizontalen Aufteilung gibt es die in der Gebäudetiefe angelegte Schichtung verschiedener Funktionsräume.

RESIDENTIAL BUILDING IN MOOSWEG, RIEHEN
Construction 2017–2019

The most prominent characteristic of this two-storey new building is the rooftop landscape that forms the exterior expression of the building's interior use zones. The main roof covers a living room, a dining room and bedrooms, while the canopy over the narrow terrace marks the transition between the house and the garden. A small rear roof accommodates all the functional and connecting rooms. Two types of layering are used inside the light timber structure of the zero-energy house: in addition to the horizontal distribution, which is characterised by living areas, the functional areas are layered towards the depth of the building.

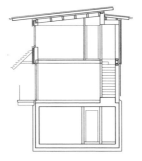

5 m

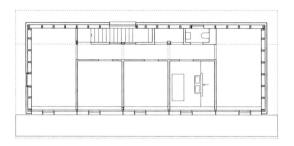

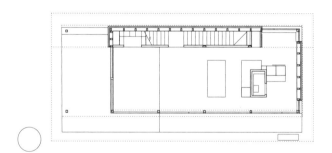

5 m

GARDEROBENGEBÄUDE, BASEL
Ausführung 2020–2021

Dieser Ersatzneubau eines Garderobengebäudes bedient zwei Nutzungen: Einerseits mussten die Garderoben- und Sanitärräume konzipiert werden, andererseits benötigte das Gebäude eine eigene Schicht für die öffentliche Nutzung während der Sportveranstaltungen – mit Steh- und Sitzplätzen auf der Terrasse sowie gastronomischen Angeboten.

Folgerichtig teilt sich der eingeschossige Holzbau in zwei Zonen. Zum Spielfeld öffnet sich eine Terrasse, die von einem signethaft in die Schräge gestellten Dach geschützt wird. Dahinter staffelt sich der abgetreppte Grundriss ins Gelände; hier sind kammerartig die Umkleiden, Duschräume und Materiallager platziert.

CHANGING-ROOM BUILDING, BASEL
Construction 2020–2021

The replacement changing-room building serves two purposes: firstly, the changing rooms and sanitary facilities had to be conceived. Secondly, the building requires its own layer for public uses during sports events, with standing and seating areas on a terrace, as well as catering services.

As a result, the single-storey timber building is divided into two zones. A terrace covered by a signature slanted roof opens up towards the playing field. Behind it, the staggered floor plan is set into the terrain; it incorporates the changing rooms and shower facilities, as well as storage space for equipment.

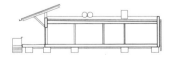

10 m

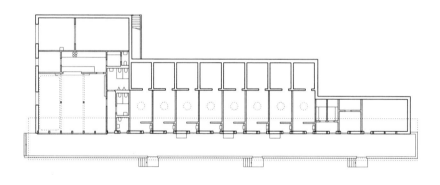

10 m

FABIO FELIPPI

1979	geboren in Liestal
1995–1996	Vorkurs an der Schule für Gestaltung, Basel
1996–2000	Ausbildung zum Hochbauzeichner
2000–2001	Berufsmatura
2001–2005	Architekturstudium an der FH Basel
2005–2006	Mitarbeit im Architekturbüro Rolf Mühlethaler, Bern
2006–2008	Mitarbeit bei Herzog & de Meuron, Basel
seit 2009	gemeinsames Architekturbüro mit Thomas Wyssen
seit 2010	Prüfungsexperte für Hochbauzeichner, Baselland
2010–2012	Assistent bei Prof. Andrea Deplazes, ETH Zürich

THOMAS WYSSEN

1979	geboren in Basel
1996–2000	Ausbildung zum Hochbauzeichner
2000–2005	Architekturstudium an der FH Basel
2006–2008	Mitarbeit bei Herzog & de Meuron, Basel
seit 2009	gemeinsames Architekturbüro mit Fabio Felippi
2011–2012	Assistent bei Prof. Marc Angélil, ETH Zürich
seit 2014	Mitglied beim Schweizerischen Ingenieur- und Architektenverein SIA

MITARBEITENDE   Elias Binggeli, Sabrina Boss, Patrick Flum, Axel Gassmann, Sybil Hofer, Elizabeth Johansson, Christoph Kirch, Vanessa Kuc, Bianca Kummer, Oliver Lenk, Elin Liden, Andreas Mordasini, Cèdric Odermatt, Jaqueline von Rooy, Selina Schmid, Julia Schütz, Eleonora Terrasi

WERKVERZEICHNIS

2010	Studienprojekt mobile Marienkapelle
	Umbau Gewerbeliegenschaft Tobler, Pratteln
	Wettbewerb Schulhaus mit Turnhalle und Aula Vernay, 1. Preis
2011	«Space in Mirror» Swiss Art Award
	Wettbewerb Schulhaus mit Kindergarten Therwil
2012	Umbau Einfamilienhaus Biascastrasse, Basel
	Umbau Hofmatt-Saal, Münchenstein
	Umbau Wohngemeinschaft Lindenberg, Basel
2013	Umbau Bauernhaus, Adliswil
	Anbau Einfamilienhaus Bärenfelserstrasse, Muttenz
	Einfamilienhaus, Dornach
2014	Umbau Villa, Sissach
	Umbau Ladenpassage Ahornstrasse, Basel
	Umbau ehem. Pfarrhaus Elisabethen, Basel
2015	Wohnhaus Baselstrasse, Muttenz
2016	Umbau Wohnhaus Leimenstrasse, Basel
	Umbau Justiz- und Sicherheitsdepartement, Basel
	Wettbewerb Kindergarten, Riehen, 2. Preis
	Fassadengestaltung Göhnersiedlung, Adlikon
	Wettbewerb Bastion Saint-Antoine, Genf, 2. Preis
2017	Wettbewerb Cycle d'Orientation, Cugy, 5. Preis

FABIO FELIPPI

1979	Born in Liestal
1995–1996	Foundation course, Schule für Gestaltung, Basel
1996–2000	Draughtsman's apprenticeship
2000–2001	Higher vocational diploma
2001–2005	Studied Architecture at the FH Basel
2005–2006	Employed at the architectural office of Rolf Mühlethaler, Bern
2006–2008	Employed at Herzog & de Meuron, Basel
2009–	Joint architectural office with Thomas Wyssen
2010–	Draughtsman's examination expert, Baselland
2010–2012	Assistant to Prof. Andrea Deplazes, ETH Zurich

THOMAS WYSSEN

1979	Born in Basel
1996–2000	Draughtsman's apprenticeship
2000–2005	Studied Architecture at the FH Basel
2006–2008	Employed at Herzog & de Meuron, Basel
2009–	Joint architectural office with Fabio Felippi
2011–2012	Assistant to Prof. Marc Angélil, ETH Zurich
2014	Member of the SIA

EMPLOYEES

Oliver Lenk, Vanessa Kuc, Elias Binggeli, Axel Gassmann, Bianca Kummer, Julia Schütz, Selina Schmid, Sybil Hofer, Cèdric Odermatt, Patrick Flum, Andreas Mordasini, Patrick Flum, Christoph Kirch, Elizabeth Johansson, Eleonora Terrasi, Elin Liden, Jaqueline von Rooy, Sabrina Boss

LIST OF WORKS

2010	Study project, mobile Chapel of St. Mary
	Conversion, Tobler industrial estate, Pratteln
	Competition, school building with sports and assembly halls, 1st Prize
2011	"Space in Mirror" Swiss Art Award
	Competition, school building with kindergarten, Therwil
2012	Single-family home conversion, Biascastrasse, Basel
	Hall conversion, Hotel Hofmatt, Münchenstein
	Conversion, Lindenberg residential community, Basel
2013	Farmhouse, Adliswil
	Apartment building extension, Bärenfelserstrasse, Muttenz
	New apartment building, Dornach
	Villa conversion, Sissach
2014	Shopping mall conversion, Ahornstrasse, Basel
	Conversion, former rectory in Elisabethen, Basel
2015	Residential building in Baselstrasse, Muttenz
2016	Residential conversion, Leimenstrasse, Basel
	Conversion, Law and Security Department, Basel
	Kindergarten competition, Riehen, 2nd Prize
	Façade design, Göhner estate, Adlikon

2017	Wettbewerb Konferenzgebäude mit Bibliothek, Posieux, 3. Preis
	Neubau Haus am Wartenberg, Muttenz
2018	Städtebaustudie Am Walkeweg, Basel
	Wohnhaus Gatternweg, Riehen
	Wohnhaus Ruppen, Muttenz
	Wettbewerb Doppelkindergarten Siegwaldweg, Riehen, 4. Preis
	Umbau Altstadthaus, Aarburg
2019–	Wohnhaus Moosweg, Riehen
	Garderobengebäude, Basel

AUSZEICHNUNGEN

2011	Foundation Award 2011, Förderpreis für Schweizer Jungarchitekten
2016	Best Architects 16 für Bauernhaus, Adliswil
	Nominierung Arc Award für Wohnhaus Baselstrasse, Muttenz
	Architekturpreis Muttenz für Wohnhaus Baselstrasse, Muttenz
2018	Best Architects 18 für Wohnhaus Baselstrasse, Muttenz
	Auszeichnung Guter Bauten für Wohnhaus Baselstrasse, Muttenz

AUSSTELLUNGEN

| 2016 | Architektur0.16, Werkschau für Architektur, Zürich |
| | Schweizweit, S AM, Basel |

BIBLIOGRAFIE

2011	Trans, Portrait Gewinner Foundation Award 2011
	Art TV, Fernsehdokumentation über das Architekturbüro
	Um dreissig, Portrait von 36 jungen Architekturbüros. In: werk, bauen + wohnen, Ausgabe 12
	Umbauen + Renovieren, ein Büroportrait
	Umbau Bauernhaus, Adliswil. In: Häuser modernisieren, S. 32–42
2015	Umbau Villa, Sissach. In: Häuser modernisieren, S. 34–39
	Wettbewerb Schulhaus mit Kindergarten Therwil. In: Grundrissfibel Schulbauten S. 13–131
2016	Schweizweit, Publikation des S AM zur gleichnamigen Ausstellung, S. 106–107
	Haus Baselstrasse, Muttenz. In: Moderne Häuser in regionaler Tradition, DVA Verlag, S. 112–117
	Umbau Bauernhaus, Adliswil. In: Best Architects, Publikation zum Architekturpreis, S. 398–399
	Portrait junger Architekturbüros um die 40. In: U40, 15 Architekturbüros unter 40, S. 72–79
2017	Bastion Saint-Antoine, 2. Rang. In: Hochparterre, Wettbewerbe 3
	Haus Baselstrasse, Muttenz, und Bastion Saint-Antoine. In: werk, bauen + wohnen, Ausgabe 1
	Haus Baselstrasse, Muttenz. In: Baudokumentation Architekturjahrbuch 2017
2018	Haus Baselstrasse, Muttenz. In: Best Architects, Publikation zum Architekturpreis, S. 146–147

2016	Competition, Bastion Saint-Antoine, 2nd Prize
2017	Competition, Cycle d'Orientation, Cugy, 5th Prize
	Competition, conference building with library, Posieux, 3rd Prize
	New house, Wartenberg, Muttenz
2018	Urban planning study, Am Walkeweg, Basel
	Residential building Ruppen, Muttenz
	Residential building in Gatternweg, Riehen
	Competition, double kindergarten, Siegwaldweg, Riehen, 4th Prize
	Conversion, old-town house, Aarburg
2019–	Residential building in Moosweg, Riehen
	Changing-room building, Basel

AWARDS

2011	Foundation Award 2011, Förderpreis für Schweizer Jungarchitekten
2016	Best Architects 16, farmhouse in Adliswil
	Nominated, Arc Award, residential building, Baselstrasse, Muttenz
	Architekturpreis Muttenz, residential building, Baselstrasse, Muttenz
2018	Best Architects 18, residential building, Baselstrasse, Muttenz
	Auszeichnung Guter Bauten, residential building, Baselstrasse, Muttenz

EXHIBITIONS

| 2016 | Architektur0.16 Werkschau für Architektur, Zurich |
| | Schweizweit, SAM Basel |

BIBLIOGRAPHY

2011	*Trans*, portrait of the Foundation Award 2011 winner
	Art TV, documentary programme on the arch. office
	"Um dreissig", portrait of 36 young architectural offices. In: *Werk, Bauen und Wohnen* Issue 12
	Umbauen + Renovieren, office portrait
	Farmhouse conversion, Adliswil. In: *Häuser modernisieren*, p. 32–42
2015	Conversion in Sissach. In: *Häuser modernisieren*, p. 34–39
2016	*Schweizweit*, publication by the Swiss Architecture Museum on the exhibition "Schweizweit", p. 106–107
	House in Baselstrasse, Muttenz. In: *Moderne Häuser in regionaler Tradition*, DVA Verlag, p. 112–117
	Conversion in Adliswil. In: *Best Architects*, publication on the architecture prize, p. 398–399
	Portrait of 15 young architectural offices aged around 40. In: U40, *15 Architekturbüros unter 40*, p. 72–79
2017	Bastion Saint-Antoine, 2nd Prize. In: *Hochparterre, Wettbewerbe 3*
	House in Baselstrasse and Bastion Saint-Antoine. In: *Werk, Bauen und Wohnen* Issue 1
	House in Baselstrasse. In: *Architekturjahrbuch 2017*, building documentation
2018	House in Baselstrasse. In: *Best Architects*, publication in the architecture prize, p. 146–147

Finanzielle und ideelle Unterstützung

Ein besonderer Dank gilt den Institutionen und Sponsorfirmen, deren finanzielle Unterstützungen wesentlich zum Erscheinen dieser Buchreihe beitragen. Ihr kulturelles Engagement ermöglicht ein fruchtbares und freundschaftliches Zusammenwirken von Baukultur und Bauwirtschaft.

Financial and conceptual support

Special thanks to the institutions and sponsoring companies whose financial support makes a key contribution to the production of this book series. Their cultural engagement encourages fruitful, friendly interaction between building culture and the building industry.

Schweizerische Eidgenossenschaft
Confédération suisse
Confederazione Svizzera
Confederaziun svizra

Eidgenössisches Departement des Innern EDI
Bundesamt für Kultur BAK

Aziri Böden GmbH,
Giebenach

Goepfert & Friedel AG,
Basel

PEVO GmbH, Arlesheim

Willi Gerüstbau AG,
Biel-Benken

Beat Joss & Partner, Basel

Holzbau Gisin AG, Lauwil

Planeco GmbH, Münchenstein

WISLERHOLZBAU

Wisler Holzbau AG,
Hölstein

ComputerWorks AG,
Münchenstein

DILL & PARTNER AG
INGENIEURBÜRO

Dill & Partner AG, Oberwil/BL

PLOTJET
Einfach drucken.

PlotJet AG, Dübendorf

z·ing

Zeuggin Ingenieure GmbH,
Basel

Cristofoli AG, Basel

Löw Gartenbau

Löw Gartenbau AG,
Muttenz

ROSENMUND
Sanitär I Heizung I Lüftung I Kälte

Rosenmund Haustechnik AG,
Basel

E. Berger & Co. Rolladen AG,
Basel

MAKIOL WIEDERKEHR
INGENIEURE HOLZBAU BRANDSCHUTZ

Makiol Wiederkehr AG,
Beinwil am See

SCHNEIDER
Gartengestaltung AG
Oberwil

Schneider Gartengestaltung
AG, Oberwil

FLÜCKIGER AG
SCHREINEREI
www.fs-schreinerei.ch

Flückiger Schreinerei AG,
Aesch

moritz-maler.ch
Begeisterung mit Farbe

Moritz AG Malergeschäft,
Augst

SwissPlan Gebäudetechnik
GmbH

SwissPlan Gebäudetechnik
GmbH, Basel

Felippi Wyssen
41. Band der Reihe Anthologie
Herausgeber: Heinz Wirz, Luzern
Konzept: Heinz Wirz; Felippi Wyssen, Basel
Projektleitung: Quart Verlag, Antonia Chavez-Wirz
Textlektorat Deutsch: Kirsten Rachowiak, München
Übersetzung Deutsch–Englisch: Benjamin Liebelt, Berlin
Fotos: Walter Mair, Basel S. 7, 9–11; Valentin Jeck, Stäfa S. 15,
17–21; Rasmus Norlander, Zürich S. 23, 25–29; Fabio Felippi,
Basel S. 31–33; Archiv Felippi Wyssen, Basel S. 35, 37–39
Visualisierungen: Felippi Wyssen, Basel S. 41, 43–45
Redesign: BKVK, Basel – Beat Keusch,
Angelina Köpplin-Stützle
Grafische Umsetzung: Quart Verlag, Antonia Chavez-Wirz
Lithos: Printeria, Luzern
Druck: DZA Druckerei zu Altenburg GmbH, Altenburg

Felippi Wyssen
Volume 41 of the series Anthologie
Edited by: Heinz Wirz, Lucerne
Concept: Heinz Wirz; Felippi Wyssen, Basel
Project management: Quart Verlag, Antonia Chavez-Wirz
German text editing: Kirsten Rachowiak, Munich
German–English translation: Benjamin Liebelt, Berlin
Photos: Walter Mair, Basel p. 7, 9–11; Valentin Jeck, Stäfa
p. 15, 17–21; Rasmus Norlander, Zürich p. 23, 25–29;
Fabio Felippi, Basel p. 31–33; Archiv Felippi Wyssen, Basel
p. 35, 37–39
Graphics: Felippi Wyssen, Basel p. 41, 43–45
Redesign: BKVK, Basel – Beat Keusch,
Angelina Köpplin-Stützle
Graphical layout: Quart Verlag, Antonia Chavez-Wirz
Lithos: Printeria, Lucerne
Printing: DZA Druckerei zu Altenburg GmbH, Altenburg

Quart Verlag GmbH
Denkmalstrasse 2, CH-6006 Luzern
books@quart.ch, www.quart.ch

* Inserted booklet with translation

books@quart.ch, www.quart.ch